Prayer and Meditation

Biblical Self-Help Tools

For Parents of Teens When You
Do not Know Where to Turn

Joan M. Blake
Key to Life Publishing Company

Scripture quotations marked "NKJV" are taken from the New King James Version.® Copyright © 1982 by Thomas Nelson, Inc. Used by permission. All rights reserved.

"Scripture taken from the NEW AMERICAN STANDARD BIBLE®, Copyright © 1960,1962,1963,1968,1971,1972,1973,1975,1977,1995 by The Lockman Foundation. Used by permission."

Scripture quotations marked "NIV" are taken from the Holy Bible, New International Version.®Copyright © 1973, 1978, 1984 Biblica. Used by permission of Zondervan. All rights reserved.

Scripture quotations marked "NIRV" are taken from the Holy Bible, New International Reader's Version.®Copyright © 1996, 1998 Biblica. All rights reserved throughout the world. Used by permission of Biblica.

Scripture quotations marked "NRSV" are taken from the New Revised Standard Version Bible. Copyright © 1989 Division of Christian Education of the National Council of the Churches of Christ in the United States of America. Used by permission. All rights reserved.

Scripture quotations marked "KJV" are taken from the Holy Bible, King James Version, Cambridge, 1769

Scripture quotations marked "NLT" are taken from the Holy Bible, New Living Translation. Copyright© 1996. Used by permission of Tyndale House Publishers, Inc., Wheaton, Illinois. All rights reserved.

Prayer and Meditation: *Biblical Self-Help Tools for Parents When You Do Not Know Where to Turn.*

Copyright © 2013 by Joan M. Blake
Published by Key to Life Publishing Company
P.O. Box 190971
Boston, MA 02119
www.keytolifepublishingcompany.com
ISBN: 978-0-9814609-4-9

Printed in the United States of America. All rights reserved. No part of this publication may be reproduced in any form or by any means, including photocopy, recording, or any information or retrieval system, without written permission from the author.

Table Of Contents

Introduction 1

1 *Accept Your Teenager* 4
2 *Assess the Situation* 6
3 *Appreciate Your Teenager* 8
4 *Be a Model for Your Teenager* 10
5 *Become Your Teenager's Best Friend* 14
6 *Be Kind to Your Teenager* 16
7 *Be Patient toward Your Teenager* 20
8 *Communicate with Your Teenager* 22
9 *Cope with Your Problems Without Attaching Blame to Anyone* 24
10 *Deal with the Major Issue Without Being Overwhelmed by the Entire Picture* 26
11 *Develop Your Teenager and Yourself* 28
12 *Discipline Your Teenager* 30
13 *Educate Yourself about the Issues* 32
14 *Encourage Your Teenager to Work* 34
15 *Establish Expectations* 36
16 *Forgive Your Teenager* 38

17 *Give Your Teenager Hope* 40

18 *Guide and Protect Your Teenager, but Do Not Force Him or Her to Do What You Want* 42

19 *Have Faith in God* 44

20 *Help Your Teenager in Times of Vulnerability* 46

21 *Listen and Pay Attention to Your Teenager* 48

22 *Love Your Teenager* 52

23 *Maintain a Positive Attitude toward Your Teenager* 54

24 *Pray for Your Teenager* 56

25 *Re-establish Your Family's Values* 58

26 *Seek Outside Help for Your Younger Children When You Go On Dates* 60

27 *Set Boundaries for Your Teenager* 64

28 *Show Respect to Your Teenager* 66

29 *Spend Time with Your Teenager* 68

30 *Teach Your Teenager* 70

31 *Wait Patiently on the Lord* 72

Introduction

Prayer and Meditation for Teens: Finding Comfort, Hope, and Purpose in the Midst of Your Storm would not be complete without a self-help booklet for parents. This booklet, ***Prayer and Meditation: Biblical Self-Help Tools for Parents of Teens, When You Do not Know Where to Turn***, includes both information that I utilized when I was raising my own four children and reflections on my own experiences with my parents. My experiences as a parent were enriching and joyful, and they came with many blessings. At the same time, some of these experiences were accompanied by tears, frustration, and anger. However, I learned to overcome these difficulties and negative emotions, and now, I am a special friend to my sons and daughters. The list of biblical tools in this book is not exhaustive, but I am confident that you will find it helpful as you deal with your teenager(s). Always remember that whatever you do for the benefit of your children will last. If you have done your best and still do not see what you had hoped for in your teenager, never feel disappointed or guilty. You gave it your best. It is now up to your child to turn things around. Love and pray for your teenager as never before; be a good listener; accept your troubled teen; and let God do the rest.

Biblical Self-Help Tools

❧ 1 ☙
ACCEPT YOUR TEENAGER

God gave your son or daughter to you to love and to nurture. Just as God accepts you with all of your faults, so you are to love and accept your sons or daughters, even with all of their failings. You should not accept their bad behavior, but you should accept them as the children of God they are.

Example

When our sons and daughters were teenagers, we did not tolerate their bad behavior. For example, at times, they stayed out beyond their curfews, and one of our children once used and wrecked our car while we were sleeping. At these times, we disciplined them for their wrongdoings. At the same time, however, we accepted them for who they were because God had given them to us.

Scripture Verse

"...having predestined us to adoption as sons by Jesus Christ to Himself, according to the good pleasure of His will, to the praise of the glory of His grace, by which He made us **accepted** in the Beloved" *(Ephesians 1:5-7 NKJV emphasis mine).*

Prayer

Lord God,

You sent Your Son, Jesus, to die in my place.

I am accepted in the Beloved.[1]

Teach me to accept my_____ (son, daughter), for who he or she is.

In Jesus' name, Amen.

---

[1] Ephesians 1:6

❧ 2 ❦
Assess the Situation

If you recognize that your teenager is going in the wrong direction, pray and ask God for help and direction. Obtain the help your teenager needs before the situation gets out of hand. Your teenager may need counseling, treatment, or medical attention.

Example

At one point, Carl and I sought counseling for our daughter, Jo-An, who, at the time, was experiencing a difficult period in her life. Speaking to someone other than her parents helped Jo-An a great deal. We also needed to find the right school placement for her. Being in the right school environment also benefited her, since the teachers in her new school possessed the skills to help her when she needed it.

Scripture Verse

"I will lift up mine eyes unto the hills, from whence cometh my help. My help cometh from the Lord, which made heaven and earth" *(Psalm 121:1-2 KJV)*.

Prayer

Father,

Thank You for giving me the understanding

That my _____(son/daughter) needs outside help.

In Jesus' name, Amen.

❧ 3 ☙
APPRECIATE YOUR TEENAGER

Do not compare one teenager to another. No two teenagers are alike.

Example

Your older daughter or son may be obedient, while your middle teenager may be a bit challenging. If this is the case, never compare your middle teenager to the older one. Never say things like, "I wish you were like your brother or sister. You are so disobedient." Doing so may make the younger brother or sister feel hurt or inferior to the older.

Scripture Verse

"Jesus knew what they were thinking. So he took a little child and had the child stand beside him. Then he spoke to them. 'Anyone who welcomes this little child in my name welcomes me,' he said. 'And anyone who welcomes me welcomes the One who sent me. The least important person among all of you is the most important'" *(Luke 9:47-48 NIRV).*

Prayer

Father,

I pray that You will teach me

To appreciate all of my children

With whom You have blessed me.

In Jesus' name, Amen.

❧ 4 ☙
BE A MODEL FOR YOUR TEENAGER

Modeling proper behavior in front of your teenager helps him/her to develop similar patterns of behavior when he/she becomes an adult. I believe teenagers tend to make positive decisions if they are taught and shown how to do so.

Example 1

Discussing issues with your teenager in an orderly manner, without yelling, is an example of modeling proper behavior in front of him/her. How you talk with your teenager teaches your son or daughter how to conduct himself/herself. For instance, if he/she only sees his/her parents argue across the room rather than discuss issues in an orderly fashion, then I believe that he/she will tend to adopt a similar behavior and lifestyle later in life. During my own childhood, I learned to speak loudly from my mother, who didn't sit us down and speak to us, but rather shouted constantly.

Example 2

Modeling proper behavior, by showing respect to your teenager, helps you in your dealings with them. Speaking to them properly tends to lessen frequent conflicts that may evolve and end up with you not receiving the respect you deserve. It is better to show kindness by saying, "Tom, can your father and I sit down with you to talk?" or "Mary, do you have time to sit with your father and me?" Showing respect like this puts them in control, because they both have to respond by saying, "yes," "no," or "not now." Unfortunately, I didn't adopt the above lifestyle with my children. Instead, for example, I would wait until my teenagers were leaving the house to remind them not to stay out too late by saying this: "You better come home on time!" Teenagers can be rebellious at times, and if you nag them, they may respond by doing the very thing that you did not want them to do.

Scripture Verse

"Don't have anything to do with **arguing**. It is dumb and foolish. You know it only leads to fights"(*2 Timothy 2:23 NIRV emphasis mine*).

Prayer

God,

I pray that

You will teach me to live in peace

And be sensitive to the needs of my family.

In Jesus' name, Amen.

❧ 5 ❧
BECOME YOUR TEENAGER'S BEST FRIEND

Allow your teenager to see your good side. Avoid being angry with him or her. Always let your child know that you are there for him or her.

Example

Become a person your teenager can trust. For instance, getting angry with Jo-An only caused her negative behavior to intensify. Working with her was never easy. However, when I allowed her to see me as her best friend by taking the time to listen to her, gently responding to her needs, praying with and for her, and reminding her that God loves her, she would trust me, smile, and tell me she loved me.

Scripture Verse

"A gentle answer turns away wrath, but a harsh word stirs up anger" *(Proverbs 15:1 NIV).*

Prayer

God,

I thank You

That Your Son, Jesus, is gentle and patient with me.[2]

I pray that I will be the type of friend to my _____ (son/daughter)

Which will help build trust in our relationship.

In Jesus' name, Amen.

---

[2] 2 Timothy 2:24

❧ 6 ❦
BE KIND TO YOUR TEENAGER

Build your teenager up; do not tear him or her down. When teenagers are rebellious, we often feel that, as parents, responding negatively is justifiable. However, speaking angrily and hurtfully to our children only makes matters worse. Remember, teenagers respond to both kind and unkind words. Kind words build them up, but unkind words rip away their self-esteem.

Example 1

Years ago, our daughter Jo-An exhibited negative behaviors as a result of her illness. When she became angry, she would throw objects across the room. When we threatened her by saying unkind words about her character, her behavior only got worse, because her self-esteem was ripped apart.

Example 2

Kind words build up your teenager. My husband, Carl, used different strategies than I did to deal with Jo-An's anger. During her outbursts, he would leave the room. When he returned, he would say to her, "Are you okay now? Go to your room now and relax, okay?" and she would obey. These kind words helped to encourage good behavior in her.

I believe that if we had taken time with Jo-An, had gently explained to her what we liked or disliked about her behavior, and helped her to understand her actions, she would not have repeated those behaviors. For example, on another occasion, when we reminded Jo-An about her behavior and taught her to control herself by counting from one to ten or by going to her room to calm down, she did not have an outburst. Kind words allow teenagers to reflect on their prior actions, and to gain understanding. Correct them by saying, for example, "I prefer that you let me know that you are angry and not throw objects around in our home. This is your home too."

Scripture Verse

"Love is patient, love is **kind**" *(1 Corinthians 13:4 NIV emphasis mine).*

Prayer

Almighty God,

Thank You for Your kindness toward me.

Teach me, Lord,

To be kind to my_____(son/daughter).

In Jesus' name, Amen.

ॐ 7 ॐ
Be Patient toward Your Teenager

We must be patient with our teenagers as God remakes them. The process of waiting is long and difficult. Even though we may often want to throw in the towel, we must be patient as we wait on God.

Example

Carl and I waited for seventeen years before we saw positive changes in Jo-An's behavior. Being patient gave us hope as we continually waited to see what God would do in her life.

Scripture Verse

"The Lord is not slow in keeping his promise, as some understand slowness. Instead he is **patient** with you, not wanting anyone to **perish**, but everyone to come to repentance"*(2 Peter 3:9 NIV emphases mine).*

Prayer

Lord God,

Thank You for being patient with me.

Teach me to be patient with my_____(son/daughter).

In Jesus' name, Amen.

⁂ 8 ⁂
COMMUNICATE WITH YOUR TEENAGER

It is important to communicate with your teenager, even if you can only say a few words of love. When your teenager is problematic, it is so easy to ignore him or her. However, what teenagers need is for you to reassure them that you love them, that you want the best for them, and that you are apologetic for anything you have done wrong. As parents, we always feel that we are right, but it may help your children respect you more if you show your teenagers that you make mistakes in the way you parent them.

Example

Even if your teenager does not wish to communicate with you, you can say something positive to him or her, such as, "I hope you had a wonderful day in school today. I love you, and God does too."

Scripture Verse

"O Lord, you are my rock of safety.
Please help me; don't refuse to answer me.
For if you are silent,
I might as well give up and die.
Listen to my prayer for mercy
as I cry out to you for help,
as I lift my hands toward your holy sanctuary" *(Psalm 28:1-2 NLT)*.

Prayer

God of the universe,[3]

Thank You

That I can turn to You in times of need.[4]

I pray that I will find time

To communicate with my_____(son/daughter)

The way I communicate with You.

In Jesus' name, Amen.

---

[3] Isaiah 42:5
[4] Psalm 66:20

❦ 9 ❦
COPE WITH YOUR PROBLEMS WITHOUT ATTACHING BLAME TO ANYONE

Do not blame your spouse for your teenager's problems.

Example

When you and your spouse experience times of stress, it can be so easy to blame each other for what's happening. Carl and I have blamed each other on numerous occasions. However, blaming does not help anyone; instead, it hinders one's walk with the Lord and tends to damage one's marriage. Instead, when you are experiencing struggles, give God thanks for giving you the strength to cope with your problems.

Scripture Verses

"May you be made strong with all the strength that comes from his glorious power, and may you be prepared to endure everything with patience, while joyfully giving thanks to the Father, who has enabled you to share in the inheritance of the saints in the light" *(Colossians 1:11-12 NRSV).*

"Let us therefore make every effort to do what leads to peace and to mutual edification" *(Romans 14:19 NIV).*

Prayer

Father,

When Your Son, Jesus, was crucified,

He blamed no one.

He said, "Father, forgive them,

For they know not what they have done."[5]

Teach me, Lord, not to blame others,

But to give You thanks for giving me peace and strength

To cope with my problems.[6]

In Jesus' name, Amen.

---

[5] Luke 23:34
[6] Psalm 68:35

🗞 10 🗞
Deal with the Major Issue Without Being Overwhelmed By the Entire Picture

Example

We faced difficult situations at times with our teenagers, but we always handled one situation at a time, because if we had looked at the entire picture, we would have been overwhelmed. For example, our son, Rese, faced legal issues at the same time that our daughter, Jo-An, faced psychological issues. We handled this hard time by focusing on each situation individually, without worrying about what would happen in the future.

Scripture Verse

"Hear my cry, O God; attend unto my prayer. From the end of the earth will I cry unto thee, when my heart is overwhelmed: lead me to the rock that is higher than I" *(Psalm 61:1-2 KJV).*

Prayer

Lord,

You know how much I can bear.[7]

Teach me to put my hands in Yours

As You lead me to quiet streams

During our family crises.

In Jesus' name, Amen.

---

[7] Isaiah 46:4

≈ 11 ≈
DEVELOP YOUR TEENAGER AND YOURSELF

Example 1

Allow your teenager to be involved in extracurricular activities. Sports and the arts are good areas for you to invest in with your teenager. I kept my teens busy with swimming and dancing. Competitions in these fields gave them opportunities to set goals for themselves and improve their self-esteem.

Example 2

While you are concentrating on raising and enriching your teens, do not forget about taking care of yourself. Utilize resources to help you deal with stress as you go through struggles. Read your Bible; join a Bible-believing church, and enjoy various activities. Join an aerobic exercise class or dance class; play golf; go fishing; listen to music, or engage in other activities that interest you. Make sure you eat well to keep your body in good shape.

My husband, Carl, swims every day because it provides therapy for him, while I participate in aerobic exercise, work on the treadmill, meet friends for tea, or take short vacation breaks. I regularly visit my favorite health food store, where I purchase foods which contain antioxidants, because they provide important nutrition for my body.

Scripture Verse

"For My yoke **is** easy and My **burden** is light"*(Matthew 11:30 NKJV emphases mine).*

Prayer

Father,

Creator of all,[8]

Thank You for carrying my burdens[9]

And giving me opportunities to relax.

In Jesus' name, Amen.

---

[8] Isaiah 40:28
[9] Psalm 81:6; Psalm 55:22

12

DISCIPLINE YOUR TEENAGER

Every son or daughter needs discipline. If your teenager is adamant about doing what he or she wants and not paying attention to the rules by which he or she should abide, it is time for your child to be disciplined. One effective method of disciplining your teenagers is to temporarily take away one or more of their privileges, such as sleeping over at a friend's home, going to the movies, or using a cell phone.

Example

Depending on your teen's age, you may be able to put the above into practice. Sometimes, however, when a teenager is older and particularly rebellious, you may have to implement other strategies to get him or her to obey you. These strategies are outside the scope of this booklet. Seek the help of your pastor or a Christian counselor to help you find the right solution for your teen's behavioral problems.

Scripture Verse

"And you, fathers, do not provoke your children to wrath, but bring them up in the **training** and admonition of the Lord" *(Ephesians 6:4 NKJV emphasis mine).*

Prayer

Lord,

I pray and ask

That You help me to implement strategies

To discipline my _____(son/daughter).

In Jesus' name, Amen.

✷ 13 ✸
EDUCATE YOURSELF ABOUT THE ISSUES YOUR TEENAGER FACES

Example

Find a support group or a therapist to work with your family. Read neuropsychological information regarding teenagers, which will help you to understand teenage development. Carl and I participated in family therapy in 1996 for three months during our daughter's attendance at her first special-needs school in Boston. As a result, we learned a great deal about our daughter's psychological condition and the steps we could take to cope with it. In addition, I formed a support group with my two friends who also had special needs children. We met at least once per month at each other's homes to discuss issues, to pray, and to support one another. Other friends, including Jo-An's godmother, would also stop over to pray with us from time to time.

Scripture Verse

"Be exalted, O God, above the heavens,
And let your glory be over all the earth.
Save us and help us with your right hand,
That those you love may be delivered"
(Psalm 108:5-6 NIV).

Prayer

Father,

Great and merciful God,[10]

Thank You for showing me that I need Your help.

I pray that I will find a support group or therapist

To work with me,

As I deal with my _____ (son's/daughter's) issues.

In Jesus' name, Amen.

---

[10] Psalm 117:2

☙ 14 ❧
ENCOURAGE YOUR TEENAGER TO WORK

A job can help your teenager develop self-esteem and independence as he or she learns responsibility under a boss instead of you. Most importantly, having his or her own money gives a teenager the opportunity to make his or her own purchases, thereby helping to ease the family's finances.

Example

As teenagers, my daughter Monique maintained jobs as a lifeguard and as a junior camp counselor during the summer months, while my sons Rese and Tony worked in supermarkets and fast-food restaurants. Money from their part-time jobs helped to defray the costs of their school clothes.

Scripture Verse

"The Lord is my shepherd; I shall not want" *(Psalm 23:1 KJV)*.

Prayer

Father,

I pray that my _____ (son/daughter)

Will find a special job

That will help _____ (him/her)

Build self-esteem and responsibility

And pay for school expenses.

In Jesus' name, Amen.

☙ 15 ❧
ESTABLISH EXPECTATIONS

Set clear expectations for house chores, school work, and how you want your teenager to treat you. Roger McIntyre, author of *Teenagers and Parents: Ten Steps for a Better Relationship*, states that teens may entertain themselves in very bothersome ways if they have no responsibilities to fulfill, no opportunities for useful activity, and no reason to expect any benefit from their choices.[11] Structure helps teenagers refrain from idleness.

Example

I made a list of household duties for our teenagers. Things went well for awhile, but eventually our daughter Monique complained that her brothers were not doing their duties, so she stopped doing hers. I believe now that giving them each an allowance would have created an incentive to get them to do their chores. We also always insisted on their doing their schoolwork, and we did not tolerate back talk.

---

[11] Roger McIntyre, *Teenagers and Parents: Ten Steps for a Better Relationship*, (Columbia: Summit Crossroads Press, 1996), 91.

Scripture Verse

"**Train up** a child in the way he should go: and when he is old, he will not depart from it" *(Proverbs 22:6 KJV emphases mine).*

Prayer

God,

I pray that my ____ (son/daughter)

Will act responsibly,

By doing _____ (his/her) schoolwork,

And the chores that I assign_____ (him/her).

In Jesus' name, Amen.

∾ 16 ∾
FORGIVE YOUR TEENAGER

You should forgive your teenager just as Jesus forgave you. Every sin your teenager has committed is forgivable.

Example

I have forgiven my teenagers for their past mistakes, regardless of whether those mistakes were intentional or out of their control. I can forgive my children, because God forgives us for all of our sins.

Scripture Verse

"Be kind and compassionate to one another, **forgiving** one another, just as in Christ God **forgave** you" *(Ephesians 4:32 NIV emphases mine).*

Prayer

My God and my Lord,[12]

I pray that You will help me

To understand my _____ (son/daughter).

Teach me to forgive_____ (him/her)

For what _____ (he/she) has done.

In Jesus' name, Amen.

---

[12] Psalm 30:2

☙ 17 ❧
GIVE YOUR TEENAGER HOPE

Regardless of the magnitude of your teenager's problems, give him or her hope. God can restore everyone's life to wholeness.

Example

While we were going through difficulties in our lives, we always felt that God was giving us hope that He would restore our teenagers, whether that meant a stable program for our daughter Jo-An to attend or establishing our other teenagers as men and women with destiny and financial stability. I always reminded my teenagers of how I came to America alone, how I researched where I would stay, and searched for a job when I got here and later enrolled in a major college. I showed them that there is hope in God through His Son Jesus Christ and that regardless of what happened in their lives, God has the power to change their lives for the better. I helped them to understand what true responsibility was and that if they lived responsible lives and trusted God to redeem their lives, He would do it. We give God praise for what He has done in the lives of our children.

Scripture Verse

"But I will **hope** continually, And will praise You yet more and more" *(Psalm 71:14 NKJV emphasis mine).*

Prayer

God,

With You all things are possible.[13]

Thank You for giving me hope[14]

That my _____ (son's/daughter's) situation will change.

In Jesus' name, Amen.

---

[13] Matthew 19:26
[14] 2 Thessalonians 2:16

~ 18 ~
Guide and Protect Your Teenager, but Do not Force Him or Her to Do What You Want

Guidance: I believe guidance should be a combination of listening and giving suggestions. Sometimes it is best to wait until your teen has asked your opinion on a given subject before giving your opinion.

Protection: Protect your teen by instructing him or her on the right way to live. However, do not force your opinion on him or her, otherwise you will push him or her away, and he or she may no longer want to share important information with you.

Example

If my teenagers confided in me and wanted my opinion, I would give them guidance concerning the matter. When my teenagers dated and asked my advice concerning, for example, the person he/she was dating, I helped him/her to analyze the positive and negative aspects of the issues he/she was facing with that individual, showing him/her that my purpose was to protect him/her, and not to force my opinion on him/her.

Scripture Verses

"He **guides** the humble in what is right and teaches them his way" *(Psalm 25:9 NIV emphasis mine).*

"They shall neither hunger nor thirst,
Neither heat nor sun shall strike them;
For He who has mercy on them will lead them,
Even by the springs of water
He will **guide** them"*(Isaiah 49:10 NKJV emphasis mine).*

Prayer

God,

I pray that You will guide

And protect my _____ (son/daughter).

In Jesus' name, Amen.

❧ 19 ❧
Have Faith in God

Have faith in God, even when things look bleak in your teenager's life. Consider and concentrate on at least one of your teenager's positive traits. Praise him or her continuously for it. Use your faith in God to help yourself rise above the difficulties that you and your teenager face.

Example

Maintain faith that your teenager will turn his or her life around. Live a life focused on what God can do rather than on the circumstances you face with your teenager. Move from hopelessness to hope, regardless of your circumstances.

Scripture Verse

"For we walk by **faith**, not by sight" *(2 Corinthians 5:7 NKJV emphasis mine).*

Prayer

Father God,

By faith I believe

That You are changing my_____(son's/daughter's) situation.

Thank You, Lord.

In Jesus' name, Amen.

❧ 20 ❦
HELP YOUR TEENAGER IN TIMES OF VULNERABILITY

During my childhood in Trinidad, or even now in America, I have seen parents abandon their teenage daughters or sons during times when they were in dire need. For example, a teenager may be pregnant and going through an emotional time and need parental support, yet be abandoned by the parent. Think of what you are doing and why you are doing it before you make a decision regarding your teenage son or daughter. There are many situations in which a teenager may feel vulnerable. Do not be ashamed of your teenager when he or she faces difficult situations. If you are unable to help your teenager, seek outside help.

Example

During tough times, I would help and encourage my teenagers by reminding them that God would heal them and restore their lives to wholeness. Carl and I felt strongly that we could not abandon Jo-An when she needed us most. We believe that God makes a way where there is no way.

Scripture Verse

"For the Lord God will **help** Me;
Therefore I will not be disgraced;
Therefore I have set My face like a flint,
And I know that I will not be ashamed"*(Isaiah 50:7 NKJV emphasis mine).*

Prayer

God,

Show me how to help my_____ (son/daughter) in times of vulnerability.

In Jesus' name, Amen.

↬ 21 ↫
LISTEN AND PAY ATTENTION TO YOUR TEENAGER

We parents always want our teenagers to excel at a particular sport or other pursuits, but what if our teenagers do not want to do what we want them to do? Listening to your teenagers is of great importance.

Example 1

I remember that at one point our son Rese did not want to continue swimming, but we refused to let him make that decision because we wanted him to swim. On the day of a swimming tournament, he refused to swim. He always played basketball in our backyard with many of his friends. To honor and encourage his interest in that sport, we could have allowed him to continue playing basketball instead of insisting that he continue swimming.

Example 2

Pay attention to how your teenage daughter responds to food and weight loss. If she is not coming to the dinner table on a regular basis, or if she is throwing up after she eats, she may be suffering from an eating disorder like anorexia. Have a talk with her, and listen attentively to what she has to say. Find her the help she needs before the situation gets out of hand.

Example 3

Pay attention to the length of time that your teenager surfs the web. There is a growing percentage of teenagers who are drawn to pornography.

Scripture Verse

"The eyes of those who see will not be dim,
And the ears of those who hear will **listen.**" *(Isaiah 32:3 NKJV emphasis mine).*

Prayer

Father,

I pray that You will teach me to listen

And to pay attention to my _____(son/daughter).

In Jesus' name, Amen.

❧ 22 ☙
Love Your Teenager

Love your teenager regardless of the wrong he or she has committed. Loving someone doesn't mean that you love what he or she has done. Follow in the steps of the Lord by giving genuine love to your teenager.

Example

I must say that love is not a choice. It is a command from God, and regardless of what we go through with our teenagers, we must make a decision to love them. We must obey God's commands.

Scripture Verse

"This is My commandment, that you **love** one another as I have **loved** you" *(John 15:12 NKJV emphases mine).*

Prayer

God,

I thank You for Your love.[15]

I confess and repent of the times

That I have been angry with my _____(son/daughter).

I ask forgiveness for my actions

And pray that I will follow Your commandment

To love my _____(son/daughter).

In Jesus' name, Amen.

---

[15] Romans 8:39

☙ 23 ❧
Maintain a Positive Attitude toward Your Teenager

Do not compare your teenager with your neighbor's teenagers or other teenagers in your family.

Example

Be excited about your teenager's accomplishments. If you can't find significant accomplishments, compliment your teenager about his or her room, pictures on the wall, his or her artwork, or how he or she looks. Your encouragement may convince your teenager to take a second look in the mirror and say, "I look cool."

Scripture Verse

"We urge you, brethren, admonish the unruly, **encourage** the fainthearted, help the weak, be patient with everyone" *(1 Thessalonians 5:14 NASB emphasis mine).*

Prayer

God,

I pray that You will help me

To maintain a positive attitude toward my _____(son/daughter).

In Jesus' name, Amen.

≈ 24 ≈
PRAY FOR YOUR TEENAGER

Prayer is our greatest tool. Prayer changes things and people. We must pray earnestly for our teenagers, especially when they are experiencing peer pressure, depression, anger, and other emotional difficulties.

Example

When things seemed out of my control, I turned to God, Who was able to turn my teenagers around and give me strength.

Scripture Verse

"Therefore I say to you, all things for which you **pray** and ask, believe that you have received them, and they will be granted you" *(Mark 11:24 NASB emphasis mine).*

Prayer

Father,

I pray that You will change my _____(son/daughter) in all aspects of _____(his/her) life.

Help____(him/her) to draw closer to you, Lord.

In Jesus' name, Amen.

~ 25 ~
RE-ESTABLISH YOUR FAMILY'S VALUES

Do not compromise your values, even when they conflict with your teenager's.

Example

When I was a teenager, my parents would always say, "I brought you into the world, but I didn't make your mind." This meant that my parents had instilled good behavior in us, but if we strayed from that good behavior, the problem was not with them, it was with us. They maintained their family values at all costs.

Scripture Verse

"For God has not given us a spirit of timidity, but of power and love and discipline" *(2 Timothy 1:7 NASB).*

Prayer

God,

I have stood by the values You have given me.

Now, Lord, show me

How to re-establish these values with my teenagers at home.

In Jesus' name, Amen.

❧ 26 ☙
SEEK OUTSIDE HELP FOR YOUR YOUNGER CHILDREN WHEN YOU GO ON DATES

Do not make your teenager care for your younger children. Making your older daughter or son the babysitter for your younger children has serious consequences. First, your teenager may be forced to give up a fun activity to help you or may feel left out of his or her group of friends. Brenda Lane Richardson and Elane Rehr, authors of *101 Ways to Help Your Daughter Love Her Body*, explain why you should not allow your daughter to be the live-in baby sitter. These authors believe that girls who are forced to take over child-rearing duties and become "little mothers" are often resentful of their responsibilities and of having been chosen for the work because of their sex. Since the parents are so busy, the child can lose her connection with them and feel abandoned. And because of her domestic responsibilities, she may not have time for friends or to simply be a child. Making matters even more difficult, younger siblings in her care may also become angry over their parents' absence and take their anger out on the sibling in charge.[16]

---

[16] Brenda Lane Richardson & Elane Rehr, *101 Ways to Help Your Daughter Love Her Body*, (NY: Harper Collins Publishers, 2001), 157.

Example

Our teenagers were all two years apart, except for Jo-An, who was six years younger than Monique. We hired outside babysitters for the first three children. When Monique went off to college, Jo-An was the only one left at home, but we did not rely solely on our adult children to care for her. Instead, we hired a personal care attendant to come in to care for Jo-An if we needed to go out. If we went on a short vacation, a personal care attendant would also care for Jo-An, and two of our adult children would volunteer to help alongside the attendant.

Scripture Verse

"For the LORD giveth **wisdom**: out of his mouth cometh knowledge and understanding" *(Proverbs 2:6 KJV emphasis mine).*

Prayer

Father,

Thank You for showing me

How angry my _____ (son/daughter) gets

When _____ (he/she) is forced to care for _____ (his/her) siblings.

I pray that I will act with fairness and wisdom

And hire help for my younger children.

In Jesus' name, Amen.

≈ 27 ≪
SET BOUNDARIES FOR YOUR TEENAGER

Providing the proper guidance and protection for your teenager will involve setting boundaries for him or her. Boundaries may include rules about how late to stay out, where to go for parties, with whom to associate and driving privileges. These issues should be discussed and agreed upon via a signed contract to show your teen that you are interested in his or her welfare and safety.

Example

While setting boundaries may be a bit challenging, it is important to have frequent conversations with your teenagers to educate them about safety issues, dating policies, sex issues, and drug abuse temptations they may face. You should be clear about your expectations in these situations. Let me give you an example. On weekends, my teenage daughter was always going to the mall or to the movies. As a safety measure, I suggested that she should be in the company of two or three friends. I would drop her and her friends off at the mall or at the movies and pick them up at a reasonable time. At times, she would travel with two or three friends by train to the downtown shopping mall. When my teenagers attended parties at their friends' homes, I cautioned them not to drink alcohol or drink from anyone's glass. I established a curfew of 11 p.m. for my teenagers to return home. We often talked about boyfriends and girlfriends, but I never really had deep discussions with them regarding sex issues or drugs. They knew the guidelines that we had established, and in some instances, they abided by them. I tended to know my daughter Monique's friends, as well as my sons' Tony and Rese's friends.

Scripture Verse

"'For I know the plans I have for you,' says the LORD. 'They are plans for good and not for disaster, to give you a future and a hope'" *(Jeremiah 29:11 NLT)*.

Prayer

Father,

Give me strength

To set boundaries for my teenager

And not give in to ____(his/her) demands.

In Jesus' name, Amen.

❧ 28 ❧
SHOW RESPECT TO YOUR TEENAGER

Do not use your authority to disrespect your teenager. I have seen in my own life that when a parent shows respect, the teenager does the same in return. Your teenager has a mind of his or her own, so respect your teenager's feelings and opinions. You can make suggestions, but you should not impose your views.

Example

I attend church regularly, and when my adult children were younger, they accompanied me to church. However, today, I do not force them to attend church if they do not want to.

Scripture Verse

"**Respect** everyone. Love your Christian brothers and sisters" *(1 Peter 2:17 NLT emphasis mine).*

Prayer

Dear Lord,

Teach me to show respect to my_____(son/daughter).

I pray in Jesus' name, Amen.

❧ 29 ☙
SPEND TIME WITH YOUR TEENAGER

Are you so busy at your job that you do not have the time to communicate with your teenager? If so, that is a huge problem. Instead of staying busy all the time, spend a few nights at the dinner table talking with your teenager and finding out what he or she is doing at school. Get interested in his or her extracurricular activities by attending a game or event in which your teenager is involved and talking about it with him or her afterward. When you are interested in your teenager to that extent, you improve your teenager's self-esteem and his or her relationship with you.

Example

Take your teenager for a walk and talk about what is on his or her mind. While on vacations, our daughters and I would walk to an ice cream store or sit on the beach and talk about issues they had in their lives. Also, my husband and I spent a lot of time with our teenagers when they had basketball games, swimming, or track tournaments. Being at their events boosted our teenagers' morale and improved their relationship with us.

Scripture Verse

"Behold, how good and how pleasant it is for brethren to dwell together in unity!" *(Psalm 133:1 KJV).*

Prayer

Dear Father,

I confess my busyness and my unwillingness

To spend time with my_____(son/daughter).

I ask forgiveness for my busyness

And ask for Your help

As I step out to spend time

And communicate with my_____(son/daughter).

In Jesus' name, Amen.

❧ 30 ❦
Teach Your Teenager

The Bible is firm about parents' responsibility to train up a child in the way he should go, and it promises that if parents do so, when the child is old, he will not depart from that way.[17] Maybe your teenager feels that he or she is too old to hear the Word of God, but use opportunities to read Scripture passages at the dinner table or discuss how to live the Christian life anyway. Also teach your teenager about how to take care of his or her body by eating the right foods and exercising on a regular basis.

Example

Even when I was busy, I would recite a psalm or pray with my teenagers regularly. I would also teach them about nutrition and how to take care of their bodies.

---

[17] Prov. 22:6

Scripture Verses

"Thy **word** is a lamp unto my feet, and a light unto my path" *(Psalm 119:105 KJV emphasis mine).*

"Or don't you realize that your body is the temple of the Holy Spirit, who lives in you and was given to you by God? You do not belong to yourself..." *(1 Corinthians 6:19 NLT).*

Prayer

God,

Thank You for Your Word.

It is a lamp to our feet.[18]

I pray that I will teach

And educate my ____(son/daughter) about loving You

And about exercising and good eating habits.

In Jesus' name, Amen.

---

[18] Psalm 119:105

❧ 31 ❧
WAIT PATIENTLY ON THE LORD

He is your help in the time of trouble. Wait until the Lord brings about change in the difficult situations you are facing. However, only you know the extent of the issues your teenager faces, so act with wisdom.

Example

I have waited patiently on the Lord many times, and He has answered my prayers. I waited seventeen years to get stability in our home and now, our daughter Jo-An attends a day program five days per week and is stable. Our son Rese has seen miracles in his own life. He is married, owns his home and barber-shop business. Our son Tony graduated from college, owns his own home, is married, and has a family. Our daughter Monique has also graduated from college with advanced degrees, has a great-paying job, owns her own home, and is newly married.

I make the above statement not to boast in any way, but to let you know that although I had my days when I suffered terribly, I also had times when I experienced joy while raising my children. I waited patiently for God to bless me, and He has. God has blessed me during times of pain and during times of joy. We do not know why we suffer; only God knows. Enjoy your life in the midst of pain. Do not wait for joy to occur before you enjoy life. God has given you abundant life to enjoy and to use to make a difference in the life of someone else. There is no better place to start than with your family: your husband or wife, and with your children and extended family.

Scripture Verses

"I **waited patiently** for the LORD; and he inclined unto me, and heard my cry"*(Psalm 40:1 KJV emphases mine).*

"Praise be to the God and Father of our Lord Jesus Christ, the Father of compassion and the God of all comfort, who comforts us in all our troubles, so that we can comfort those in any trouble with the comfort we ourselves receive from God" *(2 Corinthians 1:3-4 NIV).*

Prayer

Lord,

I praise and exalt Your name.

Thank You for never leaving or forsaking me.[19]

Thank You for comforting me during difficult times.[20]

Thank You for Your faithfulness to me.[21]

Thank You for renewing my _____(son's/daughter's) life.[22]

I can never thank You enough

For what You have accomplished in my family's life.

In Jesus' name, Amen.

---

[19] Psalm 139:7-10
[20] 2 Corinthians 1:3-4
[21] Psalm 36:5
[22] Romans 12:2

Books and Publications

To purchase Books and Publications by author Joan M. Blake, visit our website at: www.keytolifepublishingcompany.com or mail to Key to Life Publishing Company, P.O.Box 190971, Boston, MA 02119.

Prayer and Meditation: Biblical Self-Help Tools for Parents of Teens When You Do Not Know Where to Turn
COST $7.95 PLUS TAX AND SHIPPING.

Prayer and Meditation for Teens: Finding Comfort, Hope, and Purpose in the Midst of Your Storm
COST $24.95 PLUS TAX AND SHIPPING.

Prayer and Meditation: Finding Comfort, Hope, and Purpose in the Midst of Your Storm
COST: $17.99 PLUS TAX AND SHIPPING.

Standing on His Promises: Finding Comfort, Hope, and Purpose in the Midst of Your Storm
(PAPER BACK) COST $14.99 PLUS TAX AND SHIPPING;
HARDCOVER $22.99 PLUS TAX AND SHIPPING.

www.ingramcontent.com/pod-product-compliance
Lightning Source LLC
Chambersburg PA
CBHW050605300426
44112CB00013B/2079